broken

True Stories of Broken
Lives Restored

New Life Assembly

Published in Beaverton, Oregon, by Good Catch Publishing.
www.goodcatchpublishing.com
V1.1

Printed in the United States of America

Acknowledgements

Composing this incredible book was an adventure larger than any one person. I want to commend the team who worked so diligently with persistence and determination in seeing this book through to completion. As in many projects, there are hidden obstacles and unknowns that are encountered, and to the credit of this team, they had the ultimate goal of completion in their hearts and minds that now allows you to experience the power of life change found in these pages.

This project entailed many different levels of involvement. I first want to thank our Senior Pastor, Bob Wine, for his visionary leadership in recognizing the power of life-giving hope in such a book and putting his blessing upon it. I also want to express my deep appreciation to the individuals who became vulnerable enough to open their lives to the world and allow the personal stories of their past and present to be told, so that many would have the opportunity to read them and find real hope. Their names are mentioned at the beginning of each chapter.

This special book would never have been completed without the extraordinary leadership of our project manager, Angela Prusia. She led the team with excellence and empowered them to give the best that they had to offer. In addition to Angela's contribution, our team of creative writers included: Steve Brodine, Kim Clark, Toni Harvey, Anne Johnson, Lori Sizer and Deb Thee. I thank each of them for sharing their God-given gifts with us! Every story in this book was preceded by a personal interview with these respective individuals, and I want to take this opportunity to honor those who helped in that proc-

broken

ess: Todd Gregory, Mike Kelley, Mandy King, Elizabeth Peshek, Gary Potter, Sharon Stelling, Jan Stover and Pat Winters.

These stories were brought to an extra level of excellence thanks to the editors and proofreaders: Sandy Dop, Dan Fong, Sandy Fong, Jonelle Wendt and Connie Wine. Thank you for those final, refining touches. A big thank you goes out to my personal assistant, Angie Sizer, for keeping this project organized with all the "behind the scenes" work.

Faithful people like those whose names have been mentioned are making an impact with their lives that will last far beyond the years spent on this earth. May God's blessing rest on them all!

In loving gratitude,
Jeff Baker
Missions Pastor

Introduction

by
Pastor Bob Wine

Hope … based on reality. We desperately need hope that comes from knowing of someone who has "faced a lion" and not only survived, but has found new life and the ability to share that new life with others.

The stories in this book that offer hope have not been modified or dramatized, nor exaggerated or inflated. They are stories of real people who either made less than ideal choices or were victims of insensitive and sometimes savage forces that brought them some of life's greatest difficulties. Their reports are wrenching, yet 100% true. In some cases, names have been changed to protect related parties from embarrassment by being unnecessarily exposed.

The fascinating part is how these broken people were able to make decisions that resulted in authentic life change. The individuals to whom these things happened are not idols, nor perfect people. They don't ride off into the sunset, never to encounter difficulty again. Rather, like everyone else, their past is like a haunting shadow and can still exert its influence in unguarded moments. Yet, in the midst of that, they have learned to overcome and press on by refocusing their attention on who transformed them—God.

We at New Life offer these real-life stories, hoping to inspire and encourage you in your life's journey.

Content

Finishing the Race

Jay Isaac's Story
Written by Toni Harvey

The finish line blurred as the sweat ran down my forehead and stung my eyes. "Just a little further," I told myself. "You can do it; just keep pushing."

I had run this quarter-mile track many times before. I had all the confidence in the world that today would be a day of victory for me. The gunshot rang through my ears. We were off. I bounded from the starting line with all the force I could muster. The excitement and thrill of competition overwhelmed me. Aided by the rush of adrenaline, I quickly gained a substantial lead over the other runners.

It was always my speed and my long, lean physique that gave me an edge over the other runners in dashes and sprints. I had an almost hyper energy that propelled me forward. Long distance was my challenge.

My heart pounded. My legs tightened. I tried not to focus on the position of the other runners, but rather on the finish line. I could imagine the cheers of the spectators. My feet pounded on the track, responding to my will to win.

As I neared the finish line, I could feel the other runners gaining on me. How could they be picking up speed at this point? Every muscle and organ in my body cried out, "Enough!" A sickening realization swept over me. Victory evaporated. How could I have forgotten?

broken

This was a one-mile race, not a quarter-mile. I was so focused on finishing first and getting that quick lead, I forgot to pace myself. I should have started at a comfortable stride. Then, in the end, I would have had the strength and stamina needed to thrust myself forward in the last quarter-mile and cross the finish line victorious.

How could I have been so stupid? A wave of nausea swept over me. I knew I would never be able to finish this race. Something deep inside me told me to quit, but I knew I couldn't. I may have been foolish, but I was not a quitter. I couldn't let my team down. They depended on me. If I gave up now, it would affect not only the ranking, but also the morale of the whole team. To finish this race, I would have to rely more on mental strength than physical. I could recover from the disappointment of unrealized expectations, but not from the disappointment in myself if I quit.

As I watched one runner after another pass me, I forced myself to focus on finishing. I demanded that my legs keep moving, and somewhere from deep inside, I found the strength to go three more laps around the track. How I missed the most crucial piece of information concerning this seemingly insignificant race, I'll never understand. But that day, I discovered the strength deep inside me that would see me through the most difficult trials of my life. Thankfully, I did not know what obstacles lay ahead of me.

My life growing up was pretty typical for any young boy raised in the rural town of Elgin, Nebraska. I was number seven in a family of ten children. My father worked hard at a seed mill, and we rarely saw him during harvest season. My mother managed the affairs of the household and taught us the fear of the Lord. With a houseful of siblings, we were never bored. Our days were spent with whatever mischief we could conjure up.

Before I entered my teen years, my family moved to Gibbon, Nebraska, but the move wasn't traumatic for me. We saw less of Dad because of the long workdays during harvest season, but the extra income provided bigger allowances for us kids. We also stopped going to church regularly, but that meant more playtime. I didn't have a worry in the world. I looked forward to my future with great anticipation.

What the future brought me was young love. Before I turned 18, I met, fell in love with and married the one I thought was the girl of my dreams. Unfortunately, during that time, I did not have much guidance from my parents. My father was put on disability after back surgery, and as a result, suffered from depression and started to drink heavily. He was never abusive toward our family, but his absence from my life began to leave a very definite void. My mother trusted me and expected me to live with whatever consequences my choices might bring. In this case, the consequence of marrying too young was a woman who took her affection from me and decided to give her heart to another man. I was left completely alone and heartbroken.

In an effort to save my marriage and hold onto the

woman I loved, I sought counseling at my local church in Gibbon. It was during a church service there that I gave my heart to God and began to feel the power and comfort of His presence in my life.

My wife was not interested in church or in saving our marriage. She wouldn't go to counseling, so we divorced by the time I turned 19. My life was not playing out the way I had planned. Completely devastated, I cried out to God. I sought guidance from my dad. He asked me how long I was going to wallow in self-pity. Although his words seemed harsh at the time, they were spoken with love. I have since come to realize that my dad's lack of affection and participation in my life was not because he did not love me. Instead, he was not able to give what he had not been given. I began to understand that my life was not over. Mercifully, I did not know what my life had yet to bring.

Growing up, my mother always told me that God had a plan for my life. Maybe that is what kept me pushing forward when life seemed to lose its meaning. The summer after my divorce, I went out for a night of fun with my brother-in-law. He had been drinking heavily, so I took his motorcycle home.

Rain made the roads slick. Combined with the oil on the highway, conditions were hazardous for traveling. I lost control and swerved, then bounced off a culvert. I flew 50 feet through the air and crashed into a ditch.

Fortunately, a vehicle traveling behind me saw the accident and immediately called an ambulance. I drifted

Finishing the Race

in and out of consciousness, and three days later, I was airlifted to Denver. I tried to understand what was happening. I saw my mom. My dad was crying. I struggled to put my thoughts together. I remembered the motorcycle, the rain and the pavement. I felt so strange. I didn't move, and I didn't regain full consciousness until after those first three days.

The Holy Spirit brought to my remembrance the words of my mother from my youth. "Jay, God loves you. He has a plan for your life, and He will always be with you."

These thoughts drowned out the words of the doctor as he said, "Jay, you can't move your legs. You'll never walk again."

I celebrated my twentieth birthday learning to use a wheelchair. My back was broken mid-chest and my spinal cord severed. I had no feeling from my mid-chest down.

People ask me if I am angry about what happened. Every day I'm faced with the same decision I faced in the quarter-mile race I wanted to quit. Should I give in to self-pity? Regret? I must persevere, even in the face of extreme challenge.

During this time, it was the peace and comfort of my Heavenly Father, which confirmed my mother's words. I knew God's plan for me had not changed just because I had made unfortunate choices. He could still accomplish His purpose for my life. Just like that fateful race, I knew I would have to set my heart on the goal, take

broken

my eyes off my circumstances, and focus my energy into fulfilling the plan God had for my life.

Life has not always been easy, but God has always provided everything I need. The greatest blessing of my life was given to me after my accident. Her name is Linda, my wonderful helpmate and the true love of my life. My wife and I married two years after my accident. God also provided a job for me with employers and co-workers who expected me to function as a productive employee. I was not given opportunities to use my handicap as a means of invoking sympathy.

Within one year after I started working again, my older sister died of cancer, leaving eight children and a husband who was not capable of caring for them. My wife and I decided to raise the five youngest children so they would not have to be separated.

Parenthood has definitely not been without its challenges. Watching the trials my children have overcome, I understand that we are all in the race of our lives. We all face challenges, but it is how we deal with those challenges that determine if we will be victorious. How do we impact the spectators of our lives? Do we inspire them to cheer us on or to cringe with embarrassment at our poor sportsmanship?

I have watched my children suffer loss, devastation and discouragement, and then pick themselves up and continue to race. While most of them are serving the Lord, I know I must continue to pray for those who are struggling to stay on course. When I love them unconditionally, this love will push them forward when circumstances tempt them to give up.

Halfway through my race, I don't know what obstacles lie ahead, but I know I serve a God who is faithful to provide all I need. My prayer is that I will run in a way that encourages others to do the same.

> *"Do you not know that in a race all the*
> *runners run, but only one gets the prize?*
> *Run in such a way as to get the prize."*
> *1 Corinthians 9:24*

Anguish

Julie Hofer's Story
Written by Angela Prusia

"It is not ... the experience of loss that be-comes the defining moment of our lives ... it is how we respond to loss that matters."

Gerald L. Sittser,
A Grace Disguised: How the Soul Grows Through Loss

"Come on, Joshua." Brian tugged on the sleeve of his little brother's turtleneck. "Wake up. I wanna play."

Joshua's arm fell back, rigid beside his small frame. He looked so handsome dressed in his red, plaid overalls. The white satin lining of the coffin highlighted his pale skin.

I pulled Brian away. Tears blurred my vision as my gaze fixed on the body of my son. I stroked Joshua's cheek. One of his favorite Matchbox cars, a cement mixer, lay beside him. I knew I should also bury the little pickup truck with the missing wheel and the car with the worn paint, but I couldn't. Those two toys especially bore the marks of my son's love. He had clutched them in his hands wherever he went.

"Joshua's gone," I whispered into Brian's blonde hair. How could I comfort my son when my own grief overwhelmed me?

Brian took out the pig book he'd chosen earlier and tucked the gift close to Joshua's face. The story was

23

one I'd read over and over to my sons before bedtime. Did Brian think of death as sleep? What better gift could he give his brother than his favorite bedtime story?

I pulled Brian close. If only my two boys could chase one another around our home again. Raising two energetic boys was busy but rewarding, with lots of smiles and hugs. Two and a half years apart, Brian and Joshua were inseparable.

In the quietness of the mortuary, my husband and I tried to explain Joshua's death to Brian. How could he understand when even I didn't? Brian would only be five the day after the funeral. Why did his brother have to die?

Scenes from the past two weeks played through my mind like a surreal movie in which I was a character. Surely, I'd been given the wrong script. A part of me listened to the words of the doctors and made funeral arrangements with the mortician, while another part of me slipped away.

Joshua was a healthy child. When he got sick after our trip to Colorado with my parents, I wasn't worried. I took him to the doctor and was told Joshua had a virus. Four days later, on a Sunday, I called the doctor in the middle of the night. Joshua wouldn't stop coughing. The doctor figured he had croup. By the next morning, Joshua was in the emergency room. He could hardly breathe.

Joshua had tracheitis, an infection of the windpipe. It was a rare disease, similar to bronchitis or pneumonia, only the infection settled higher.

By Monday afternoon, Joshua had a tube inserted

down his throat to keep it from swelling shut. Joshua was admitted to the ICU and placed on a respirator. To keep him from pulling his tubes, Joshua was given a paralyzing drug.

Throughout the day, I felt little anxiety. Our church family lifted us in prayer. My faith was strong. I knew God would bring healing to my son.

Things worsened Monday evening. Joshua suffered a traumatic fit of coughing. In a moment of panic, his tube was pulled. Because of the infection, his throat swelled shut and the tube could not be reinserted. Joshua received a tracheotomy so he could breathe through his neck with a respirator, but not before he had been without oxygen for twelve to fifteen minutes.

Perhaps because of our ignorance, neither my husband nor I fully understood the extent of our son's illness. Little clues slowly formed a picture I wanted to deny. His body became rigid, a condition known as posturing. As Joshua's organs began to shut down, his blood pressure dropped, and he had trouble with digestion.

Our church covered Joshua in prayer. The call went out to others in different states, even to the Fiji Islands, where my cousin and her band of friends prayed. Our pastor and his wife led a group in prayer at the church, while two elders, their wives and my parents prayed with Joe and me over Joshua. I asked God to heal my son, but promised that if He didn't, I would serve Him anyway. This prayer helped set the attitude of my heart, even though I didn't really believe God would take my son. In the Psalms, which I had always thought to be a bit melodramatic, when David says he will fear no evil, I assumed no evil would come.

What felt like evil did come. Joshua died one week after he'd been admitted to the hospital. My husband and I made the difficult decision to donate Joshua's organs, then waited with him until the transplant team arrived. After the surgery, I held my son's still warm body. I felt like I could suffocate.

Holding Brian as I tried to explain his brother was gone, I felt old and tired. Without warning, the family I had planned, the children spaced so evenly apart to be the perfect playmates, was a family of three. I mourned the loss of my ideals for Brian, the innocence lost, the grief that would change the face of his childhood.

Seven years after Joshua's death, I still miss my little boy. Simple things make me smile or cry when I think of him. I wonder about the older woman and the eleven-year-old boy who benefited from Joshua's kidneys and liver. Does the woman radiate Joshua's sweet nature? Does the boy carry Joshua's energy and passion onto the ball field? Does a mother somewhere smile when she hears her son say, "I love you, Mama?"

When Joe received a job transfer to Kearney, I didn't want to move. No one there would know my son, Joshua. I was devastated, yet I knew the move would be best for our family.

God is faithful. Our life in Kearney has provided us with a new start, a time to heal. God has given us a

church family we love and has used us in ministry. He added to our family with our children, Caleb and Bethany. The two have brought a balm to our hurting hearts. Brian was so excited with Caleb's birth, he told everyone, including strangers, about *his* new baby even eighteen months after Caleb's arrival.

God brought us through the dark days that followed Joshua's death, despite the whys I couldn't answer and the moments I wanted to change. When two miscarriages followed, I couldn't understand why God would allow so much pain into our lives, but I clung to my faith. The pain was too great to waste. If I had to drink from this cup, I did not want to emerge from my pain as a bitter, angry person.

I don't know that I'll ever understand why Joshua had to die at such a young age, but I now understand the anguish that made David cry out to God. I, too, can say, "I will fear no evil, for You are with me." In light of eternity, my life is but a moment. I have learned to trust God to shape me, whatever the circumstances.

The Ditch or the Path

Greg Wengert's Story
Written by Anne Johnson

"Come out with your hands up!"

I bolted upright. "What the…"

The red and blue lights from a cruiser flashed in my dresser mirror. I slipped out of bed and crept to the window.

"What is it?" my girlfriend whispered.

"Cops, lots of them."

I scanned the room. "Oh, no." I dove across the bed, scrambled toward the dresser and crammed the plastic bag full of white powder into my pillowcase.

"We're coming in."

Before either my girlfriend or I could answer, we heard a large thud. Wood splintered as it fell to the ground.

"So much for the front door," I said.

I turned to Melanie, who sat silent on the bed, her eyes wide as a deer.

Lights burst into the darkness of our home as uniformed men invaded.

"Hands up." An officer pointed a gun at me. "Keep them where I can see them."

"Greg, do something," Melanie protested.

Like ants on a sandwich, the officers searched our house. At gunpoint, Melanie and I were forced to wait on the couch in silence. Am I dreaming? This can't be hap-

broken

pening.

The drug bust seemed to take all night. My arms ached as I tried to relax my fists. How had my life come to this?

"You can pick up your weapons next week," an officer finally said. I couldn't believe it. The police found nothing. No drugs.

One by one, the officers left. In unison, the doors on the patrol cars slammed shut. The flashing lights stopped.

I eyed the debris around me. Every cabinet was opened, every drawer searched. Clothes and dishes littered the floor.

"Let's go back to bed. We'll clean up tomorrow," I said.

"What?" Melanie screamed. "How can you sleep after that?"

I shrugged. "What's the big deal? They didn't find anything."

"That's not the point," Melanie said.

Her eyes filled with tears. Great, no sleep tonight. We sat on the couch for the rest of the night. Melanie talked and cried. I tried to pay attention, but my mind continued to wander. How had they missed the pillowcase?

I fell asleep with my arms around Melanie. The events of the night slipped from my mind.

After the raid, Melanie changed. She stopped partying with me. If we talked at all, we would end up in

32

a fight. She worked extra shifts and saved all she earned, but the worst change was church.

"Please come with me to church," Melanie said.

"I did the church thing when I was young," I said through clenched teeth.

"Greg," Melanie's eyes bore into mine, "it's more than going to church."

I didn't let her finish. "You go. But leave me out of this Jesus craze."

And she did. She left me. I did not know what hurt more, her leaving or my parents taking her in.

Lost, I sat alone. I never knew silence could be so loud. I looked around the house and realized I had nothing. My life had no meaning. I wanted to die. What was there to live for? I spied the full bottle of Jack Daniels on the table. Quick fix. But I craved more. I wanted Melanie.

I ran out the door. The slam of the screen door was muffled by the hailstorm of thoughts that pelted my mind.

I hadn't run in years. Winded, I gasped for air. Night surrounded me, a multitude of stars my only companion.

Miles down the road, I slipped on some loose gravel and slid face first into the ditch. The dry corn stalks from the surrounding field crackled in the wind. I shook my fist at the night sky. "Why? Why did You let her leave?"

Silence. Had I just yelled at the sky? Was I crazy? Or could there be someone, something beyond the stars? I stood and turned in a circle like the pivot in the field.

My breathing slowed. I gazed heavenward. As a child, I had been forced to attend church. When my parents gave me the choice, I stopped going. Why talk to someone who wasn't there? Or was He?

"God, are You there?" I challenged.

The silence erupted into a flurry of memories. How had I gotten home all those years when my vision and judgment were hampered by the influence of alcohol and drugs? How had the charges of drug manufacturing been dropped? When I was in jail, how did the bail money get raised so quickly?

My hands cradled my face as I cried. My chest heaved. And Melanie, how had I found her? Miracles, all of them. Not my doing but . . .

"You have been there, God. You are the reason I am alive today." I stood and stared into the sky. "Forgive me," I whispered.

Peace descended over me as I lifted up my voice in prayer. I climbed out of the ditch and turned toward home.

The next week, I cleaned house. I flushed all the alcohol and drugs down the toilet. I had tried this before, only to return to this way of life with a vengeance. Not this time. To stop these habits, I would need to trust in God. Only His power could free me from my addictions.

I pushed the doors to the church open. Why was I here? For Melanie or for me? Neither. For Him. I

The Ditch or the Path

needed God. I wanted to know my sins were forgiven. I longed for God's love.

Months later, I felt my eyes burn with tears at the sight of Melanie's radiant smile. I had never seen her look more lovely than when she walked down the aisle toward me. Her white dress was an outward symbol of the cleanliness we both felt inside our hearts. God did what He promised. He forgave us. We stood before God and man, saying our vows.

Do I still fail? Yes. Will God fail me? Never. I'm learning I must die to myself, or to my sin, on a continual basis. The cravings haunt me, so *daily* I must choose to walk the narrow path with God. Otherwise, I fall on my face back in the ditch again. Without God, I am a slave to sin. Like Paul in Romans 7, I can say that, "I have the desire to do what is good, but I cannot carry it out. For what I do is not the good I want to do . . . it is sin living in me that does it . . . waging war against the law of my mind and making me a prisoner of the law of sin . . . What a wretched man I am! Who will rescue me from this body of death? Thanks be to God, through Jesus Christ, our Lord!" Jesus alone will save me from the ditch.

The Person in the Mirror

Holli Coffman's Story
Written by Kim Clark

The haunted face in the mirror gazed blankly back at me. *Just a few more pounds, then I'll stop.*

I'd already lost ten pounds, but I wasn't satisfied. The compliments only fueled my desire to shed more pounds. It was easy, just like Suzi said. We were cheerleaders and both determined to shine in our senior year of high school. I watched Suzi's self- confidence soar as she lost weight. I was not heavy like Suzi, but I was tall, which made me stick out against my shorter, smaller-boned friends. No one said anything to tease me. I just always thought I was fat.

"Gag yourself," Suzi had said when I asked her about her diet. She demonstrated how she stuck her forefinger into her mouth.

The idea of throwing up my food repulsed me, so I determined to lose weight another way. I'd eat less and exercise more.

The plan started out great. Even my mother, who was always conscious about her weight and exercise, commented on my new habits. My confidence swelled. For the first time in my life, I felt in control.

I lost several more pounds by graduation and entered cosmetology school. My high school sweetheart, John, proposed to me, and I was thrilled. I decided to lose just a little more weight for the wedding.

broken

Compliments soon turned to criticism. The more people wanted to control me, the more I dug in my heels. I was in control. I could stop dieting whenever I wanted.

My weight plummeted to a gaunt ninety-two pounds, and still I wasn't satisfied. A baked potato fed me for two or three days. Between my workouts at the gym and my physical labor at the electric hose and rubber factory where John and I got jobs, I was starving my body of vital nutrients. When I stared at the mirror, my criticism of my imperfections blinded me to the truth. Only the constant criticism from others frustrated me more than my own self-doubt. *You're too thin. You don't look good. Are you eating?*

"Fine, I'll go," I told my mother when she begged me for the millionth time to seek help. I was sick of the nagging. My sister wasn't any better. I would go for treatment just to get her off my back. I enrolled in a thirty-day program in North Platte.

Treatment terrified me. I was locked on the third floor of the hospital with other patients with eating disorders. I hated the constant monitoring. Everything I ate was recorded. When I wouldn't eat, the nurses force-fed me. I'd never been so degraded in my life. During my counseling sessions, I rebelled. I didn't need help. I was happy. Or so I told myself.

After a week in treatment, I received a weekend pass to go home, so I decided to surprise my husband. I was excited. I could actually have fun since it was the Fourth of July weekend. When I couldn't find my husband at home, I went to the festivities downtown. I wasn't prepared for what I saw. My husband was with another woman and her child. Their perfect family didn't include me. I was so overwhelmed, I left with a girlfriend as my Cinderella-like dreams collapsed around me.

I returned to treatment a different person. For the first time, I was open to treatment. I worked hard to deal with my issues of hurt and anger; I needed to gain the strength to handle my life circumstances when I went home. By the end of the week, I convinced my counselor that I needed to be home to deal with issues regarding my husband.

John and I had been married almost ten years. We had started dating during my sophomore year of high school. He was the only one I confided in about my home life. He became my closest friend, and I spent most of my free time with him and his family. They were kind and generous, and I felt accepted when I was with them.

Looking back, I now understand my eating disorder was a vain attempt to gain power over the emotions raging within me. From the time I was a little girl, I searched for ways to escape the reality of my life. When I was two, my dad died in a plane crash. Two years later, Mom remarried, and we moved from Minden to McCook. My step dad had three other children, but they only stayed with us occasionally, so I never developed a strong relationship with them. I felt like an intrusion in my step dad's life. He could tear me apart with his words. Mom and I were close in the beginning of their marriage, but

41

broken

drew apart as time elapsed.

When I was in the fourth grade, we moved to a farmhouse about twenty-five miles from Culbertson. My feelings of isolation grew since I lived so far away from town. Because of the emotional distance I felt with my parents, I became more lonely and insecure.

As I remember that time of my life, I am still overcome with sadness. Memories of my childhood don't include playing to have fun. My parents expected me to be responsible at a very young age, but I lacked a sense of direction and often felt like a lost, little girl looking for something outside of my reach. I spent a lot of time alone in my room, in a fantasy world, pretending.

In junior high, I coped with my feelings of low self-esteem and loneliness by participating in volleyball and cheerleading. I often stayed at friends' homes overnight. My friends' parents made me feel like part of a real family. At my home, I wasn't allowed to show emotions or express my feelings, but at my friends' homes, I could be myself.

My family moved into an older house that was closer to town when I was a freshman in high school. On the night of my junior prom, an electrical fire destroyed our home. We lost everything we had. I had nothing to wear but the prom dress I wore. I felt such a total sense of loss and wondered what we would do. Where would we go? Thankfully, no one was in the house when the fire started, but I lost the only memento I had from my fa-

42

ther—a cherished heart-shaped diamond ring he'd given my mother. She'd passed it on to me just a few years before. We later dug through the debris, searching for anything we could salvage. Nothing remained but ashes.

We lived in a simple trailer on the site until we could build a new house. My older stepbrother lived with us during that time. He was involved in drugs and alcohol and often came home drunk. I was filled with anger and frustration toward him and his lifestyle. When voices got loud and arguments came, I escaped to my room.

My step dad was well known and respected in the community, but we didn't talk much about what went on at home. I was so lonely, I wanted to run away. I took advantage of my freedom once I was old enough to drive and left home whenever I could to get away from the turmoil.

If only I could drive away from my problems with John. Instead, we divorced, and I soon exchanged one addiction for another. Two weeks of treatment for my eating disorder weren't enough to break my chains.

Alcohol consumed every waking moment. It was a constant burden, yet an insatiable need. Soon after my divorce, I began to date a man who was successful and well liked. I moved to Kansas City to be with him. He was a controlling person, and the influence of alcohol in my life allowed him to control me. I didn't know anyone in the city, and I turned to alcohol on a daily basis, even while I worked. I tried to hide my addiction, but my boyfriend found out and committed me to a rehab hospital. I

hated being back in treatment. I didn't want to get out of
bed or be around anyone.

When I sobered up, I found a new life. I became
faithfully involved in Alcoholics Anonymous. Through
AA, I met some of the most awesome people I have ever
known. I felt at home among the other people who were
just as sick as me. One of the counselors, Maggie, a beautiful, redheaded woman, took me under her wing. My
spiritual advisor, Eric, told me about Jesus Christ. I asked
Jesus into my heart and began to experience a freedom
and peace I had never known. I cried out to God to save
me from my path of self-destruction. I started to read the
Bible and prayed continuously for Him to keep me free of
the compulsion to drink, and He did. When I left treatment, I knew what I had to do to live a life without alcohol. I attended AA daily and quit my job at the beauty
salon to work in a church daycare. I ended my relationship with my boyfriend. Now that I was sober, he didn't
like my lack of dependence on him.

I didn't know much about God when I was growing up. The only real Christian influence in my life was
my grandma. I had looked forward to summertime when I
could stay with my grandparents in their little house on a
farm. Grandma played dress-up with me with her old
clothes in the attic. We made mud pies or worked together in the garden. She even taught me how to bake and
crochet.

Two years after I became sober, my grandpa
passed away and I moved back home to help my grandma.

44

I continued attending AA and worked two jobs. Grandma and I spent most of our evenings at home together, just the two of us. She shared more with me about God and His Word. I had lots of questions about my faith, and she always had an answer. She brought to life what I had already learned about God when I was in treatment.

While I lived with my grandma, I met Randy, who is now my husband. I moved to Kearney when we married, and we found a new church home at New Life Assembly. Through our involvement in the church, we both grew in our faith and developed a deeper relationship with Jesus.

Randy and I were told we would be unable to have children, partly due to the abuse I had put my body through. For a year, I prayed to accept the idea that I would never have a child. Then I found out I was pregnant. Randy and I were both absolutely astonished! Our daughter, Sarah, was truly a miracle and a gift from God. She continues to be an incredible blessing to me. The pull of my addictive nature returns at times, but motherhood and the awesome responsibility of caring for my daughter have kept me from falling back into my old habits.

My step dad and I went through a process of healing. We have a good relationship now. After going through counseling, I forgave him and stopped blaming him for my issues and the choices I made. I also found healing from the grief of losing my dad when I was a little girl.

I stand amazed at what God did in my heart. He

lets me know I am loved and so special to Him. This year, I started to pray for God's priorities in my life. The process has humbled me to realize I am special, regardless of my past or what people think. Nothing else matters, but that He accepts me.

Today, I have a passionate relationship with God. The daily struggles no longer threaten me. I know He is with me every day and will pull me through the tough times. I desire to know Him more, so each morning I spend a quiet time with God in prayer where He reveals something new to me every day. God wants to make me into the person He created me to be. He allowed me to experience circumstances in my life so I could grow and learn to trust Him.

When I find myself struggling with a difficult situation, God is there. Even in the darkness, He gives me hope. When I choose to put Him above every issue in my life, I can rest assured that nothing in life will happen that He won't help me through.

> *"The LORD Himself goes before you and*
> *will be with you;*
> *He will never leave you nor forsake you.*
> *Do not be afraid; do not be discouraged."*
> *Deuteronomy 31:8*

Resurrected

Carmen Urwiller's Story

Written by Anne Johnson & Angela Prusia

I watched the truck leave before I grabbed my suitcase. Sounds of the argument between my youngest teenage son and my husband still rang in my ears. I couldn't even remember what started the fight. All I knew was the utter hopelessness I felt.

Clothes landed in haphazard fashion as I tossed them into my suitcase. My need to leave overshadowed my need to be perfect.

Tears stung my eyes as I backed the Suburban out of the driveway. My husband, Gary, would understand; he knew I needed help. My son, Brian, would not.

I made it as far as the Byco service station in Grand Island, twenty-five miles away, when I turned back. What kind of mother was I? I needed to say goodbye first.

I gripped the steering wheel. What was wrong with me? I was 50 years old, blessed with a wonderful husband and four children. To those on the outside, I was June Cleaver, complete with the plaster smile and spotless apron. I was a Christian, so why wasn't I happy? Why did the slightest thing set me on edge?

When my husband returned, I poured out my heart. I confessed that I'd called a counseling crisis helpline I'd heard about on Christian radio. Though Gary knew I'd been unhappy, he had no idea of the depth of my despair. How could he? We made arrangements for me to go to

broken

Tulsa, Oklahoma, to Brookhaven Hospital (now one of the New Life Clinics with Dr. Stephen Arterburn).

A week later, I found myself on an airplane, headed for . . . *a mental hospital?* On a scale of one to ten, I felt like a big fat zero. Nothing. Worthless. Of no value to anyone, not to myself, not to my family, not even to God.

Checking into a mental hospital both terrified and humiliated me. If I'd broken my leg, I would've seen a doctor, but this was different. I believed the lie that depression came from some hidden unhappiness or conflict in my life. I didn't understand the chemical deficiency within my brain. Nor did I understand I had a genetic predisposition to depression.

My daily routine was reduced to eating, sleeping and taking care of myself. I was no longer the busy mother, the bookkeeper, the errand runner, the housekeeper, the decorator, the peacemaker and every other role I performed. I was simply Carmen, whoever she was. I was placed in a "family" with rebellious adolescents, survivors of child abuse and people addicted to drugs and alcohol. What exactly was *my* problem, anyway? I had a faithful husband who loved me and provided for our family, I didn't drink or smoke, and I tried to honor God in my daily life. It was almost more depressing to see I had no reason to be depressed. Though suicide was not an option, death seemed more desirable than an endless stream of bleak and hopeless days.

I was the "nice guy," the personality type who is

self-sacrificing, overly conscientious and dutiful, a perfectionist and very religious. This person, I learned, is more likely than any other to get depressed at some time in life. When I wrote out my personal history, I began to see the amount of stressors I had experienced, especially in the five years from 1979 to 1984.

I gave birth to a child.

Gary and I adopted a three-year-old, and made the trip to Central America to bring him home.

My father was ill, without diagnosis, for a year. He died the day before my fifteenth wedding anniversary.

My father-in-law, who farmed with us, had a heart attack with subsequent quadruple by-pass surgery.

We helped my in-laws move to a different house.

My mother had thyroid cancer surgery.

We endured a church split, which included much personal pain.

I purchased a floral shop, which my husband and I completely remodeled.

I attended six weeks of floral design school, five hours away from home.

Our three school-age children changed from public to private Christian school, requiring forty-five miles of driving each day.

I was hospitalized with ulcerative colitis. Five months later, I was taken to the emergency room with a bleeding kidney, an indication of cancer. I had my left kidney removed at a later date.

Prices for commodities plunged in the midst of a

terrible farm economy. The value of farm real estate, which was our collateral, suffered. The interest on our farm-operating loan skyrocketed to eighteen percent.

Through counseling, I discovered I was in need of God's grace just as much as anyone in that hospital. My problems may have seemed insignificant in comparison, but the problems were very real to me. Seeing God as my Father, who understands and cares for me as His child, was a lesson I needed to learn.

I had grown up fearing God, but I didn't understand that Jesus died for my sins and wanted to reconcile me to my Heavenly Father. The Christian counselor who worked with me gave me a set of tapes entitled "Measuring How Much You Matter to God." Since I had spent our first session discussing the kind of marriage I desired, I wondered what my worth had to do with my marriage. Until I began to listen to the tapes, I didn't realize that every part of my being—physical, mental, emotional, social and spiritual—had to do with how I felt about myself and my relationships.

I discovered my self-worth, my feeling of significance, is essential to my emotional, spiritual and social stability. I saw myself as Gary's wife or Christy's mother, even the person in church who does the decorating. I never realized my true worth, my identity. I am a daughter of the King!

I had to retrain my very thought processes. God wasn't interested in my acts of righteousness, but in my personal relationship with Him. Freedom is in Christ. I had the scripture in my head, but not in my heart. I didn't believe His Word was true for me. His light began to cast away the darkness that depression imprinted upon my life.

In Second Corinthians, Paul pleads with God to take away the thorn in his flesh, but God says, "My grace is sufficient for you, for my power is made perfect in weakness." The same is true in my life. Though I've learned to control my depression through medication, the study of scripture, and with help and prayer from support groups such as *Turning Point Ministries*, the thorn still pricks me.

I lost my mother two years ago. A conflict broke out within our family over the estate. A year later, my nephew was murdered. After returning from his funeral, we learned my father-in-law had a stroke and had to be moved into a nursing home. These events triggered a major episode of depression in my life, something that hasn't happened since my treatment eleven years earlier.

I would love to say my thorn no longer hurts, but I can't. However, because I know I am a daughter of the King, I can rest in His embrace. Like Paul, "I will boast all the more gladly about my weaknesses, so that Christ's power may rest on me. That is why, for Christ's sake, I delight in weaknesses, in insults, in hardships, in persecutions, in difficulties. For when I am weak, then I am strong."

"I have loved you with an everlasting love; I have drawn you with loving-kindness.
I will build you up again and you will be

broken

rebuilt.. .again you will take up your tambou-
rines and go out to dance with the joyful. "
                    Jeremiah 31:3-4

Around the Next Bend

Jim Reier's Story
Written by Steve Brodine

When I fell into the flooded Platte River, I knew I was in trouble. The icy, cold water soaked through my clothes and numbed my skin. I opened my eyes and saw the green, murky mess churn about me. My head broke the surface. I grabbed for a branch.

I caught a twig no bigger than my pinkie, but at least I had something to hold. The rushing water roared past my ears. I looked downriver and saw nothing else to grab. I only saw another bend in the river, and I didn't need more surprises. The water was too swift, too deep and too cold already. I knew if I let go, I'd be dead, catfish bait.

A wave of relief rushed over me as I felt two hands grab my coat and pull me from the raging water. To this day, I don't know how my rescuer saved me, but I will be forever grateful.

I was only a teenager then, and I couldn't imagine I'd ever experience anything as terrifying as that again. I had no way to know how the twists and turns of that river would be like my life. I had much to learn as I grew up in Cozad, Nebraska.

One of my earliest memories involves my father. When I was four years old, I was playing on a haystack with some neighbor kids when someone pushed me, and I fell off. I still remember the dull, sick feeling in my stom-

broken

ach from the pain. When I cried, my dad said, "Shut up, you little sissy, and get in the pickup." Later, I found I had broken my collarbone, but worse than that, I had a broken spirit. I don't remember crying for years after that. Perhaps that's why I grew up feeling distant from God. I believed God, like my father, must be waiting for me to mess up, then he'd let me have it.

As I grew, I did well in sports and fell in love with a girl I met through martial arts. Her parents talked to me about knowing Jesus, and I met Him a week before we wed. While some emotional healing began to take place in my heart, I wasn't ready for Jesus to be Lord of every part of my life. Now that I was married, I figured life was smooth sailing, especially with the birth of our three children.

My life, like the flooded river, turned sharply when my wife told me she wanted a divorce. We had our share of struggles in our marriage because we both wanted control, and I felt as hopeless as I felt that day in the river. After years of stuffing my emotions deep inside me, I cried again.

God threw me a life preserver when I counseled with Pastor Wine. He helped me refocus and see I had an opportunity to model my Christian walk for my kids. Not only did I start to pray for my kids, but I took an Insight Class at New Life Assembly, where I learned I needed to forgive. I struggled until I finally let go and let God. The bitterness and anger I held in my heart left.

I eventually started going to a Friday night group

with other single adults. That's where I met Marilyn. I had been a Christian for a number of years, but she came into my life as a baby Christian. While I had lost a lot of the spark and flame of my Christian walk, she glowed with the enthusiasm new life brings. I realized for the first time in my life that God is good, and I saw He could take the pieces of my broken life and put them together again. Marilyn and I dated for two years, and then we married.

We had each suffered a great loss and that drew us close. She survived the suicide of her husband, while I lived through the pain of my divorce. We started a ministry to ride motorcycles for Christ, and the river of our life broadened as we began to reach out to others. We shared our stories with others through the Christian Motorcycle Association (CMA). "Jesus carried us through our hurts," we told others. "Jesus was the reason we made it through." People knew we were open and real with them.

Bikers respected us since we earned our colors in our CMA system. For example, I earned my colors by watching a tape series on how to be a servant, then applied the messages in real life. I learned how to listen to others so I could earn the right to be heard. There's a brotherhood among bikers that many Christians could learn from. Of course, they do wrong things like all of us do, but there are a lot of things they do right.

Once again, I enjoyed the calm, smooth sailing I so desired. I didn't know the next sharp twist in the river of my life loomed so soon ahead. One Monday night, I went to the gym after I got off work. When I got home, I saw Marilyn sitting in front of the TV and cheering for the St. Louis Rams and Kurt Warner, an outspoken Christian. She was his number one fan. As I fixed my sandwich, she started hollering and screaming.

"What's going on?" I asked as I walked into the TV room.

"St. Louis just scored a touchdown. Now we're less than a touchdown behind." I went back to the kitchen. She started screaming again. "You're not going to believe this. St. Louis intercepted and ran the identical play as their last touchdown, and they got another to go ahead."

"Awesome," I said, as I sat next to her. Out of nowhere, she made an odd noise I had not heard before. I turned and looked to see her hands clutched and crossed across her chest. I jumped up and grabbed hold of her. Marilyn focused on me, then just as fast, her look became vacant.

Frantic, I dialed 911. The ambulance unit came within a matter of minutes and took Marilyn to the hospital.

Pastor Wine met me at the hospital, and I told him I thought things would be okay. I figured it would be lack of faith to say otherwise. When a man in scrubs called my name, Pastor and I followed him into a quiet room.

"We tried several procedures," the nurse said. "We began to work on her immediately." His forehead wrinkled. "But when the first procedure did not work, then we went to the second and then…"

"Wait a minute," I interrupted. "She's not going to make it?"

"I'm sorry," he said. His eyes filled with tears while mine began to flood. "Her heart stopped."

I was drowning, not in the river, but in my own devastation. Marilyn had more heart than anyone I knew. She was only thirty-three years old, so young, so vital, so alive.

How do I convey all that flashed through my mind? Among the flood of pictures and emotions were vivid recollections of our memories together. Times when we laughed together and cried together. Times when she made me feel special. Awkward moments, intimate moments. Her perfume lingered in the air. Our songs played in the background. A lifetime of love in a few short years. I don't pretend to understand—and earlier in my life, I wouldn't have had the same thought—but in a flash, I knew I was happy for her because she was in heaven.

My assurance came from watching someone so passionate in her walk with the Lord. Marilyn and I learned so much together about our purpose for living life here on earth. Out of gratitude to God, we could reach out to others. Seeds she planted in my life, and in the lives of so many others, will continue to grow and reproduce.

As I began to drift further down the river, I could look back and see how God lifted me out of the murky mess of my life and saved me. I see how God shapes me for His purposes. I have a peace that passes my understanding.

broken

In the process of healing me, God restored my relationship with my dad. The strain of feeling distant from him when I grew up is gone. Now my dad and I are so much closer. We talk every week, and when we get off the phone, we both say, "Love you."

I continued to seek where the river would take me and found a new branch, where I can minister to others who have lost their spouses. While I pursued this ministry, God brought a unique, beautiful woman, Nancy, into my life. She has her own story of how she lost her husband. Nancy became a Christian, and I've been privileged to watch her grow as she puts roots deep into His river.

Nancy and I got to know one another better and eventually fell in love and married. I am eager to see where this new river will take us. We both know God is waiting for us to come home someday. Until then, we know we can trust Him, no matter what is around the next bend.

Innocence Restored

April Corbin's Story
Written by Kim Clark

"No, Daddy! No!" I screamed. My small body shook with terror. I was only three years old.

My dad had crashed through the door in a blind frenzy. His eyes were wild and bloodshot, and he reeked of alcohol. Cursing, he waved a pistol around the room. He had come looking for my mom, my sister and me. "So, this is where you've been hiding from me!" he yelled. His anger was uncontrollable. A gunshot rang out, and I heard my aunt scream. My mother's body crumpled to the floor. He swung around and fired another bullet into my aunt's chest. I watched in horror as my aunt fell next to my mother's body, and a pool of blood spread around them. My father had killed them both.

My sister and I sobbed as we huddled together in a corner. We were at the Chevyland Museum, a roadside showplace of classic cars that my uncle owned. There was a small apartment in the back of the museum. Mom had taken my sister, Star, not yet two years old, and me to stay there only a few days before to protect us from our father's drunken rages. She planned to divorce him as soon as she could save enough money.

"Get up!" My dad grabbed Star and me. He shoved us down onto the cold, cement floor and held my sister and me against his body. He raised the pistol to his temple, his hand trembling. "April, do you want Daddy to

die, too?"

"No, Daddy! No!" I cried through my sobs, but he pulled the trigger anyway and ended his life. Blood splattered everywhere, covering my sister and me.

As I struggled to free myself from his limp body, I heard a familiar voice. My cousin, Tommy, burst into the room; he was returning from celebrating his eighteenth birthday with friends and had heard the gunshots. Taking in the horrific scene, he immediately called the police. It seemed like an eternity before they arrived. Two officers grabbed Tommy and handcuffed him, assuming he was responsible for the murders. One officer carried my sister and me to his patrol car. I was shaking and tears streamed down my face. After he calmed me down, the officer questioned me. Through my tears, I told him what had happened.

My sister and I were released to the custody of our maternal grandparents, who adopted us that year and raised us as their own children, even though they were in their sixties and retired at the time. Despite all of the love and care I received from my grandparents, my childhood was also filled with other memories. Horrible memories.

Both my sister and I were molested as children. We suffered ongoing abuse for years. One time in particular has haunted me. I was ten years old when I was raped. Afterward, my abuser beat me and threatened my life if I ever told anyone what he had done. In my mind, I took ownership of the abuse. Since I thought my grandparents had adopted my sister and me to take the place of my mom, I felt I had to be perfect to prove my worth. I figured I had done something wrong to deserve this treatment. I kept the abuse a secret, partly because of my own misplaced guilt, but also because of my granddad's battle with cancer. I didn't want to further burden my grandparents.

Although my grandparents were Christians, they didn't talk about their faith. We went to church and prayed together as a family, yet I didn't understand God's role in the relationship. I thought it was a one-sided relationship, just me praying to God. When I was sixteen, I attended New Life Assembly, where I began to learn more about a personal relationship with God. I wanted to know Him personally and to receive His love and forgiveness that He promised. I began to study His Word and asked Christ into my heart. Four years later, Star also surrendered her life to Jesus.

I began to understand that for God to heal me, I had to be willing to break the silence and share with someone about the struggles I had endured. It took me almost six years to open up and share with someone about my rape. It was about that same time, I also confessed to a youth worker that I believed the death of my father was my fault. If I had just said, "No, Daddy," louder, he wouldn't have shot himself. Through prayer and counseling, I began to understand the absurdity of my belief. I was three at the time. How could I be at fault? I had believed so many of the enemy's lies. The Holy Spirit prompted me to begin trusting my Heavenly Father and

broken

the people He put in my life to help me. I had to take that difficult step of faith and accept that God really did have something more for me.

When I was nineteen, I left for Rockford, Illinois, to attend Master's Commission, a ten-month program of intense Bible study and ministry. During that time, God changed me from the inside out. He taught me how to be a little girl, something I had lost. I would go into the sanctuary of my church and feel God's arms around me, holding me and loving me. A friend gave me a little stuffed lamb to remind me that I am God's precious lamb. I carried it in my backpack for a very long time. I began to understand His incredible love for me. God also showed me I was pure in His sight. What had happened to me was not my fault. God gave me a hope that He has a beautifully orchestrated plan for my life.

When my grandfather died, I fell into a deep depression. Since my grandmother had passed away two years earlier, I felt desperately alone. In a moment of despair, I wrote a note expressing the depth of my sadness. My sister was terrified when she found the note. She assumed I would end my life. I was admitted to a psychiatric hospital for care. The experience was horrible. I lost my appetite and wouldn't eat. My roommate, an elderly lady, told me, "You're too young to be in here. You have too much life left ahead of you." I knew she was right. I had to get out of there. After a week, I returned home, and God began to heal me through counseling and prayer.

Star and I had only each other after my grandparents' deaths. I decided to enroll in cosmetology school, but I worried how I could attend school full-time. A few years earlier, I had become close with Sandy Dop, my co-drama director in youth ministry. She and her husband, Dennis, invited us to live with them while I went to school so I wouldn't have to work. For the past eight years, they have been there for my sister and me. They have three grown children of their own, as well as twins who lost their mother. Now, Star and I have a brother, sisters, nieces and nephews. We feel as though we have been adopted into their family. Dennis and Sandy even refer to themselves as "Mom and Dad" because they love us as their own children. We feel privileged to be part of their family.

Through counseling, the love of my new family and friends and much prayer, I began to realize that I had allowed myself to make many unhealthy decisions as an adult that were a direct result of the trauma in my child-hood and the lies I believed because of those events. For example, although I had tried to be discerning and actually had avoided some relationships that would not have been healthy, I allowed myself to fall into a couple of situations that were unhealthy and simply not right for me or for the other person. Other areas were also affected. I allowed employers to abuse me by demanding more of my time with no monetary compensation. And when people who really did love me got too close, I pushed them away, afraid that they might see just how undeserving I was of their love. I couldn't believe that I deserved more. I began to see these beliefs as what they were: lies of the enemy to steal my joy and to keep me in bondage to my past.

Forgiveness has been a challenge for me, whether it is forgiving myself or someone else, but God is helping me learn to forgive others and to let those hurts go. He will take care of the outcome. It took a long time for me to forgive my dad until I began to see him through God's eyes. My dad was a very sick man. He was an alcoholic, as well as a diabetic, and suffered from a depressive disorder.

Forgiving doesn't mean I have to like the people who hurt me, but it does mean that I choose not to hold their sin against them. I release them into God's hands. Sometimes I have to choose to forgive every day. Jeanne Mayo, the senior pastor's wife where I attended Master's Commission, often said, "Right choices bring right emotions." If I choose to forgive everyday, the right feelings will come. I just need to continue to trust God and allow Him to be in control of my life.

Thankfully, God has helped me to overcome my past. I had to get to the point where I didn't want to be the way I was. I had to believe that God had a plan for my life and that I really could be the person He had created me to be. Is it all over? No, sometimes things will happen that get me down, and I begin to hear those same old lies. The enemy doesn't give up easily, and he knows the lies worked for a long time. My family reminds me of who I am in Christ. The Bible says we really are conquerors in

Christ who gives us a hope and a future.

I don't always see His plan, but I've learned to give my circumstances to God. I know that God didn't want my parents to die the way they did. It wasn't something He planned, but He allowed it, and I know He will use it for His greater purpose. I have to be willing to ask God, "How are You going to use my pain for Your glory?" If I'm patient and trust Him, He will show me. Sometimes it takes years, but He always uses our pain for good. Like the calm at the eye of the hurricane, God will be our peace in the midst of the storm.

Redeemed

Stan Smidt's Story

Written by Deb Thee

"I want a divorce."

I looked at my wife, trying to decide what approach to take. We'd had this conversation before. "Come on." I pulled her close to me. "You're not still mad about the other night?"

She pushed me away. "You were dead drunk, Stan."

I shrugged.

"It was our fifth wedding anniversary." Something in her voice told me she was serious this time.

Guilt washed over me, but I felt powerless to change. I didn't want to admit what I knew to be true. I was an alcoholic.

I threatened my wife. I knew she abused prescription drugs, so I tried to hold this against her by telling her I'd take our daughter away. She cleaned up. I didn't.

Six months later, we divorced. Because I drank our money away, I had accumulated much debt. I had to sell everything, the house, the cars, the farm equipment, and I still owed the IRS $35,000. Like always, I turned to alcohol.

Looking back, alcohol was always a part of my life. I was five years old when I had my first drink at a family gathering. By ten, I was drinking brandy with my uncles when we went hunting. I was a heavy kid with low self-esteem. Alcohol made me feel good, if even for a little while. In no time, I needed to drink more to numb my pain. I got my first MIP (Minor In Possession) before I graduated from high school.

Alcohol was easy to get. Growing up in a small town, parties were common. Social lines blurred under the influence of alcohol. I went to many parties where my coaches, teachers and even cops were present.

After my divorce, I moved to Colorado. I wanted to start over, so I bought a tanning salon. My use of wet t-shirt contests for advertising only made me slide quicker into the lifestyle of drinking and promiscuity.

One relationship made me fear for my life, so I decided to move back to Nebraska. It was no surprise that I hooked up with the old gang. Soon, I was in trouble with the police. When I spent the night in jail for a DUI, I figured I had a bout of bad luck. During another run-in with the police, I had a minor car accident, but I managed to elude the cops.

Two days later, I was lying in a hospital bed, unable to move. Even though I had escaped the police, I had injured my back. A month after my back surgery, I couldn't feel anything from the waist down. I couldn't even use the restroom on my own. Talk about humbling. The doctors discovered I had a pinched nerve from the swelling after surgery.

God had been trying to get my attention for a long time, but I didn't listen until my daughter confronted me. She was ten when she told me she didn't like to be with

me when I drank. Her words broke my heart. Up until then, I'd only thought of myself. I never realized the pain I'd caused my daughter.

Quitting wasn't easy. Alcohol controlled me. I tried to avoid alcohol on the days I saw my daughter, but it wasn't long before I got a second DUI. I was in jail a short time later, but this time, I realized I needed to change.

I'd tried AA before, but after getting out of jail, I turned to the group once again. I started to hang out with sober friends, something I'd never done. We talked about a higher power and the big book, though I was clueless to what this meant. One night after an AA meeting, I felt a strong need to surrender my drinking problem to God. I returned to my rundown apartment and made sure no one was around before I got down on my knees and said my first prayer. That night, my desire to drink left. I wished I'd prayed years before.

The IRS had never forgotten my debt. I decided I couldn't avoid the government any longer, so I wrote a letter. The response was nothing short of a miracle. I received an abatement, so I owed only $1,500 to settle my debt. I couldn't believe it.

After more back surgeries, I looked into less physical occupations and found a need in the tool-sharpening business. With things looking up, life was good. Even a short but failed second marriage didn't bring me completely to my knees before God.

I met Cynthia, a recovering alcoholic, at an AA

broken

meeting. Friendship turned into a relationship. After living together for a while, we began to ask ourselves if our relationship was the best model for our teenage children. We separated. Two months passed, and Cynthia gave me a book about bondage by Dr. Neil Anderson. I began to recognize the chains on my life. I asked Jesus to come into my heart. God also took away my compulsion to smoke.

Cynthia and I began to attend New Life and later got married. Praise God! To be equally yoked with my best friend is incredible. We celebrate God's blessings every day together, big and small, including the healing God has brought to my relationship with my daughter and the opportunities to share my faith with her.

God cleaned up the mess I'd made out of my life. Now He uses my testimony to help others break free. Two areas, small group leadership and missions, are close to my heart. Through small group ministry, I'm hungry to share the freedom I've received with others. In the area of missions, I've gone to El Salvador, Mexico and Honduras. If God is willing, my work here has only begun.

When I think of how God has changed me, I can gladly boast in my weaknesses because then His strength is made perfect. Nothing else explains why He chose to use someone like me.

Journey to Freedom

Steve Adkins' Story
Written by Toni Harvey

*"For I have the desire to do what is good,
but I cannot carry it out. For what I do is not
the good I want to do; no, the evil I do not
want to do – this I keep on doing."*
                              Romans 7:18b-19

My night darkened like many had before. The room was so quiet, I wanted to scream just for the comfort of the noise. I fell to my knees. I was 16 years old, and thoughts of suicide bombarded my mind with such force that I pounded my fists into my head in an effort to drive them away. I couldn't stop my body from shaking or the tears from streaming down my face. My heart literally felt like it was being ripped apart as I recalled my actions of the day. I grieved over how many times I had done things I knew were not right. I didn't understand why I couldn't stop myself from living a life of immorality and perversion. It was not what I wanted. I didn't choose this life. I felt as if I had no control over the things that happened to me; but the one thing I knew I could control was whether I lived or died.

A tingle went up my spine and through my skin. I had the eerie sensation that I was no longer alone in my room. It was almost as if I could feel the presence of good and evil, a battle that was being waged for my very soul.

broken

As I contemplated the best way to put an end to my misery, my mind began to justify my actions. I was simply trying to play the cards I'd been dealt; I was surviving by any means necessary; anyone else in my situation would probably make the same choices I had made, maybe even worse; I wasn't really hurting anyone else, not the way others had hurt me; most people in my situation wouldn't care about anyone or anything; I wasn't a bad person. The justifications just went on and on. But then in the middle of my reasoning, the grief came back with yet another wave of emotion. If I wasn't a bad person, why couldn't I stop doing all of these horrible things? I cried out to God, "Please let me die!"

All of a sudden, the mood in the room changed, and I felt something I recognized, a feeling that I longed for night and day. I didn't want to lose it. It was a sensation of warmth and comfort, like someone wrapping a huge, warm blanket around my shoulders, and in an instant, my world was made right. I felt comfort and security, things I had not experienced growing up. I felt peace and acceptance, two things I had always desired. Most of all, I felt love. How could it be? How could someone so unlovable be loved so much? I knew I wasn't worthy of something so wonderful, so good and so pure. While I knew I didn't deserve to be loved this much, I also knew that I needed to change. The most critical thing to me at that moment was the knowledge of where this amazing love came from. I knew it came from God.

Journey to Freedom

"... I have loved you with an everlasting love; I have drawn you with loving-kindness..."

Jeremiah 31:3b

I remember hearing about God for the first time when I was in kindergarten and living with my grandparents in Dubois, Wyoming. I really liked the little Nazarene church that Grandpa would drive Grandma and me to occasionally. I especially enjoyed Sunday school, but I can't explain why I loved being in that church so much. I only know I felt a peace and a belonging that I didn't feel anywhere else. I felt like some sort of magnetic pull, a powerful force that attracted the innermost part of my being, drew me there. Unfortunately, my mom was not there to share this experience with me.

I loved my grandparents very much, and my time with them was safe and stable, but even with them and my new church, I felt very lonely and empty inside. I longed for my mother. I wanted her to hold me and tell me she loved me and that we would always be safe when we were together. I wanted her to know that I loved playing with Tonka trucks and to see the look of pride on her face when I took them apart and put them back together again, all by myself. I got a big lump in my throat as I wondered when I would see her again.

My mom had married for the first time when she was 16 years old. After being married for only a couple of years, she watched her husband drown when they were

broken

out having a day of fun on the river. Feeling lonely and afraid, she married the next man that came along: my father. Marvin was an abusive alcoholic, but my mother stayed with him anyway. Soon after they married, I was born. My given name was Melvin. For the next three months, my mom endured horrible mental and physical abuse, including severe food deprivation. She even witnessed my father kill another man. Finally, she decided that she had had enough and we left. Marvin swore that if he ever found us, he would kill us both.

My mother was so afraid of my father, and of being found by him, that she moved me somewhere new about every six months. I lived with aunts, uncles and grandparents. Most of the time, Mom and I stayed together, but that was not the case in the beginning, when I lived with my grandparents. It never occurred to me that my life wasn't normal. I just accepted that we did what we had to do. Mom sat me down often to tell me what we were doing and why we were doing it, and I didn't question her.

One day, when I was in first grade, my mom came to get me. She was married again. His name was Ron, and he was also an alcoholic. I remember watching him beat my mother with milk cartons that had been filled with water and then frozen. Another time, I watched him tie a telephone cord around her neck and try to strangle her. In the late afternoon, my siblings and I started watching the clock. We knew that when the big hand was on the twelve and the little hand was on the five, Ron would come

84

home, and he would spank us, pants down, with his two-foot machete knife. The humiliation inflicted upon us during these times of abuse was almost as bad as the physical pain that we endured. Thankfully, my mom got tired of his behavior, and we left again.

This time we went to stay with my mom's sister in Houston, Texas. A little while later, my mom married again. This man already had two sons, but only one who still lived at home. He was 17 years old. I was still in the first grade and was very excited to have an older brother. I thought that maybe now I would have someone that would take care of me and teach me how to be a man. I thought that, because he wasn't really a grown-up, he would have the time to do fun things with me. I was wrong. Right away, he began molesting me and my brothers and sister. It wasn't long before we told Mom what was happening, and we left again. Unfortunately, we went back to Ron.

Mom and Ron would stay together for a while, and then he would get drunk and abusive, so Mom would take us kids and leave again. This pattern continued for longer than I care to remember. Many nights, Mom and I lay in bed and cried. I hated Ron. I wanted him to disappear forever.

It was during this time, though, that I was given another chance to hear about God. When I was in third grade, I joined the Boy Scouts. One of our projects was to learn about several different denominations and visit various churches. I liked the Baptist church the best because the people there were so friendly.

Every Sunday in that little church, they had a "Just as I Am" call; and every Sunday, I went down to the altar. I felt like God was drawing me to Him and showering me with His peace and comfort. One time, the pastor asked why I came down to the altar every Sunday. I told him I didn't want to go to hell. I wanted to live forever with Jesus. He told me if I gave my heart to the Lord, and was sincere in my desire to live for Him, I should believe that Jesus came into my heart and washed me clean. It was not something I had to do over and over.

Just when I was starting to settle in and make friends, Mom decided that she had had enough of Ron and determined to leave him for good, so I was uprooted again. Eventually, Mom got a job as a waitress at a truck stop, and we were able to rent our own house. Since we were on our own now, I became the man of the house. I was only 11 years old, but Mom and I made all of the decisions together. We counted our money and decided what groceries to buy, and I was responsible for my brothers and sisters while Mom was at work. There were five of us kids now. After we moved away from the Baptist church, I didn't go to church again for a very long time.

"Be self-controlled and alert. Your enemy, the devil, prowls around like a roaring lion, looking for someone to devour."

I Peter 5:8

When I was in sixth grade, I began to feel a different kind of pull on my life. In the same way that I responded to the pull I felt when I was drawn to the Baptist church, I began to respond to this new pull as well. This time it did not lead to peace and security. Now it was as if I was being bound and dragged in a direction that I had no desire to go, and I didn't know I had the power to resist it.

I don't know if it was because I was so involved in the affairs of our household and wanted to help with the financial provision, or if I was just trying to find my place to fit in, but I began to feel the need to bring home some money. I was able to get a job at a carwash down the street and felt good that I would be bringing home a paycheck. Shortly after I began working there, the owner, who was an older man, asked me if I wanted to make some extra money. I couldn't believe my good fortune. Not only was I making my own money at twelve years of age, but I also had an opportunity to make even more money than I expected.

Eager to find out how much I would be making, I went to the home of my boss like he told me to do. Immediately, it became clear that the extra money he referred to was going to come from sexual services provided to him. As the realization of what he expected from me began to sink in, my knees began to buckle. I felt like someone had punched me hard in the stomach. This couldn't be happening. If I could only open my eyes, the nightmare would go away. But I was awake. A trap had been set for me, and I couldn't get out of it. Not only was I faced with the possibility of losing extra income, but I also knew that my job was on the line. So I submitted to his requests, and the vile abuse continued until I was almost sixteen years old.

When I was still in sixth grade, my mom met and married Harold Adkins. Harold was a nice man, but he worked in the oil fields, and we didn't see him much. A few times he came home drunk, but he was not abusive. Mom was tired of the alcohol, so she and Harold worked things out, and he never came home drunk again. Harold really wanted to make us a family, so he adopted all of us kids. Finally, we all had the same last name.

I had been going by the first name of Steve for a while, even though my name was Melvin. Every time I moved to a new place, I called myself by a new name. I had fun reinventing myself. My aunt once told me she thought I looked like a Steve, so that was the name I used most often. When Harold adopted us, my mom told me that since we were changing our last name, I might as well change my first name. So I officially became Steve Adkins.

For reasons I've never understood, I was always being presented with one indecent proposition after another from boys and men. After one of our moves, I thought I had finally met a group of guys who were going to be my friends. But I eventually found out that they only wanted me around so they could force me to do lewd things. I knew even then that I liked girls and that the kinds of things I was doing with guys was wrong, but I felt powerless to stop. On top of these pressures, I also had groups of boys who took pleasure in beating me up about once a month.

When I finally admitted to myself that the relationships I was involved in were not real, I began to spend more and more time alone. My grades in school dropped to D's and F's, and I only went to school two or three days a week. On the days that I did decide to go to school, I made sure that I was drunk or stoned or both.

In seventh grade, I got tired of getting beat up and started to fight back. In the first quarter of my seventh grade year, I was expelled and sent to an alternative school. I used anything I could to fill the void in my life. I took drugs, drank alcohol, sniffed paint and stole money wherever I could find it. The only thing I respected was anything having to do with God. I didn't steal from anyone if I thought that they were Christians, and I was uncomfortable around the guys when they used the Lord's name in vain. I didn't know why it made me so uncomfortable. I only knew that when they talked like that, I felt guilty and ashamed.

When I was fifteen, my cousin and I stole some checks, forged them and ended up in court. My aunt and uncle agreed to take me into their home to keep me out of jail. They had become born-again Christians, and they took every opportunity to talk to me about God. I eventually did begin to cry out to God, and that is what brought me to that night in my bedroom. I didn't want to keep disappointing Him.

broken

> *"Therefore, there is now no condemnation for those who are in Christ Jesus, because through Christ Jesus, the law of the Spirit of life set me free from the law of sin and death."*
>
> Romans 8:1, 2

Soon after that night, my uncle invited me to attend a men's conference with him at church. It was at that conference that I experienced a greater transformation. I again prayed the prayer of salvation, but this time, I truly had an understanding of what that meant, and I was making the commitment to actually follow Christ and acknowledge Him as my Savior. I now felt like my life had meaning and purpose. I also prayed for the baptism of the Holy Spirit at that conference and received not only my prayer language, but also a new power and boldness I had never felt before.

I would like to say that my life since that time was without sin, but I cannot. I can say, however, that because of the power of the Holy Spirit at work in my life, I never again felt the same bondage to sin like I felt before. I was able to discern things more clearly, and I had the ability to stand against things I felt were wrong. I never had another physical relationship with a man from that point on. Unfortunately, other lifestyle changes did not come as easily.

Growing up, I had a habit of always asking about my real father. Mom made it clear that he was not her favorite topic of conversation. One day, we were at a gas station when she looked at me funny and asked me if I still wanted to meet my real dad. When I nodded, she pointed at a man across the parking lot and said, "He's right over there." I went over to the man and told him who I was. That day, my father and I began the process of getting to know one another.

Marvin was remarried and had three children with his new wife. He told me that if I would drink with him, he would buy all the alcohol I wanted. Because I had always wondered about my dad, and so badly wanted his acceptance and approval, I took him up on his offer. This paved the way for me to fall back into some of my bad habits and renew relationships with some of my old so-called friends.

I found myself in trouble with the law again at the age of seventeen. This time, the judge told me I had the choice to stay with my aunt and uncle and get my high school diploma from the alternative school, or I could go to the state penitentiary. I realized I had a choice about the direction of my life. I began to understand there were serious consequences to my irresponsible actions. I also began to realize that the peace I found when following after Christ could not be replaced by any other person or thing. I decided to stay with my aunt and uncle and get my act together. I graduated three months ahead of schedule.

broken

"Do not be yoked together with unbeliev-ers. For what do righteousness and wicked-ness have in common? Or what fellowship can light have with darkness?

2 Corinthians 6:14

My aunt always told me that somewhere out there, God had a girl especially for me. I found it hard to be-lieve that there could be one person created especially for me, and it was even harder to believe that I would know her when I met her. Then one night it happened. I was out with friends when a car with two girls pulled up next to ours. Two of my friends began fighting for the atten-tion of the blonde, but I liked the redhead. The others told Amy and me to make a beer run, so we left. Instead of going to the liquor store, we went to a parking lot and talked for hours about what we thought made a good mar-riage. We both had ideas about what we thought a good marriage should and shouldn't be. That night, we learned enough about each other to know that we wanted the same things from a mate. The only problem for me was that Amy didn't know Jesus.

Given my lifestyle, it seems crazy that I would hold others to any kind of standard, but I knew I could never marry anyone who wasn't a born-again believer. The only happy marriage I had ever witnessed was that of my aunt and uncle. I also noticed that when I was around other believers, I became the best part of myself. But when I was around my non-believing friends, I reverted back to my old, sinful ways—to that life I knew I didn't want.

Early in our relationship, Amy's father passed away. Soon after his death, her mother decided to move to Washington. Amy didn't want to leave me so her mother encouraged us to move in together. We were happy that we were able to be together, but we never felt comfortable living together before marriage. I had encouraged Amy to give her heart to the Lord, so she agreed to go to a Mike Warnke crusade that was being held at the local high school. I was not able to go with her, so she went with my mom. At that crusade, she asked Jesus to come into her heart and be the Lord of her life. Soon after that, we were married.

> *"Do not conform any longer to the pattern of this world, but be transformed by the renewing of your mind."*
> *Romans 12:2*

Through the course of several years, Amy and I had good jobs, nice things and two beautiful daughters. Even with all of these things, we couldn't help feeling that something was missing in our lives. We tried to get involved in church, but we never felt like we were being built up in our faith. It wasn't until God brought us to Kearney, Nebraska, that our spiritual walk began to change.

We came to Nebraska to help my aunt after my

uncle and cousin were killed in the oil field. She told us about Kearney, so we came here looking for a job and found two. One day when I was out running errands, I noticed New Life Assembly. I went home and told Amy and the girls that there was a church we needed to visit. When we came here, we were so overwhelmed with how kind everyone was to us and how quickly we were accepted and encouraged to get involved. As we began to attend church regularly, we began to feel strengthened in our faith. We attended a Crown Financial Class that changed our perspective about material possessions. I went on several mission trips and developed some strong friendships with other men in the church. I even started working at the church. The biggest boost to our spiritual walk, though, probably came when we were invited to attend an agape group, a small, in-home Bible study.

Al and Nancy Hammar became mentors to us. Under their guidance, we really began to grow spiritually. We began to hear the Word of God, read our Bibles, memorize scripture and discuss with other Christians what we learned. Then we felt the transforming power of Christ at work in our lives. We worked through a study called *Experiencing God,* which was life-changing for us. We realized the more we sought God by hearing and reading His Word, the more He spoke to our hearts and made clear to us what we were supposed to do with our lives. For the first time, we felt certain we were right where God wanted us to be. We had a vision for our future and an assurance that our lives had meaning and purpose. I felt like I had arrived home after a long, hard journey. After being discipled by others in the church, Amy and I grew to the point where we were ready to start leading our own marriage group. It gave us great joy to feel like we finally had something to offer. We were so thankful for what we'd been given, we wanted to make the same investment into someone else's life that had been made into ours. Knowing we can impact someone else's walk with the Lord gives our life meaning.

> *"... the Spirit helps us in our weakness.*
> *We do not know what we ought to pray for,*
> *but the Spirit Himself intercedes for us with*
> *groans that words cannot express."*
>
> *Romans 8:26*

There are some nights when I still find myself alone in my room, on my knees, with tears streaming down my face. But now I am not grieving over my own sinful nature, but rather for loved ones, friends and acquaintances that haven't yet found freedom from the bondage of sin in their own lives. I pray that they will repent and make a commitment to live for Christ. I pray that they will see the truth of who they are, based on what God says about them in His Word and not based on the circumstances of their lives. I pray that through the sharing of my story, others will be guided to the path that God has laid before them so that their own journey to finding freedom may be enlightened.

95

broken

I cry tears of joy for a loving, Heavenly Father, and I thank Him for bringing me home.

> *"Your word is a lamp to my feet and a light for my path."*
>
> Psalm 119:105

A Miracle

Bonnie Payne's Story
Written by Angela Prusia

"I can handle anything the doctors say," I said, with more conviction than I felt. My voice caught as I glanced over at my husband and saw his knuckles grip the steering wheel. "Just not cancer," I whispered.

I stared out the window without seeing anything. It was good that I wasn't the one driving to Children's Hospital. My senses registered information—the chill to the early spring day, the steady hum of the heater in our little Cutlass, even the faint smell of my husband's after-shave lotion—but nothing stuck. I felt like a used piece of Scotch tape. Too much had been thrown at me, and I kept trying to use the same strip of tape to hold everything in place.

My three-day-old daughter whimpered in her car seat. My own tears rolled down my cheeks. This was supposed to be a happy time, just like it had been two years earlier with the birth of our son. Jason had been healthy. Kristin was not. She'd been born fifteen days early and appeared normal, but the doctor discovered something was wrong with her bowel and bladder functions. Though the ultrasound revealed nothing, the MRI showed a mass on Kristin's spine.

"Please don't let it be cancer," I pleaded with God

for the millionth time. Not only had both my grandmother and mother fought cancer, but my sister now battled the disease. Things didn't look good for my sister, Laurie. Kristin was only a baby. I couldn't imagine facing the same pain with her.

"Should we pull over?" My husband's voice was strained.

"Huh?" For a second, I'd forgotten my baby was crying. What kind of mother was I?

Jim repeated his question. His face was ashen. I knew he was terrified. "Why Kristin?" he'd asked. "Why not me?"

"She's probably hungry," I said, as I stared at the back of her infant seat. Even basic needs had taken on new meaning. Spit-up and dirty diapers, even sleepless nights, were a welcome sacrifice compared to this nightmare. If only my daughter could be healthy. I cradled Kristin's small body in my arms and did the only thing I could. I nursed her. Even that would be restricted after midnight. The doctors wanted to take a biopsy.

A biopsy on my baby? I tried to push away the fear and listened to Kristin's sweet suckling sounds. A tiny fist wrapped around my finger. I memorized her perfect face, the soft eyelashes, the curve to her lips and her small ears. "Please, God. Let her be okay."

The test at Children's Hospital confirmed my worst fear. Kristin had neuroblastoma. The cancer had grown in my womb, starting on Kristin's adrenal gland and growing into her spine. The doctors needed to perform

surgery the following day.

The news came like a death sentence. The next several hours were filled with countless tests and interviews with the doctors. Children's Hospital is a teaching hospital, and I got tired of retelling Kristin's story to every resident and intern who walked into our room. The green color that engulfed the sixth floor mocked me. Television annoyed me. I felt lost. Fear clawed my insides. God never seemed so distant, especially since neither of our families could come to Omaha. Only when Stan Mast, a friend from New Life Assembly, showed up at the hospital did we feel God remind us of His presence.

The lingering fear of surgery darkened the day. Kristin wouldn't stop crying. It had been seven hours since she'd eaten, and every new test upset her more. I'd never felt so helpless. My tears mingled with Kristin's when I heard that our pastor and his wife, Connie, were on their way.

I'll never forget the moment Connie took my wailing child from me. She held Kristin close to her and rocked her, soothing her by praying God's Word over her. Kristin became peaceful. Before Kristin's surgery, Pastor prayed with us. He told us he felt the presence of angels surrounding us.

I held onto Kristin's hand as the nurse wheeled her to the operating room. My heart sank when the sliding doors to the OR shut, separating me from my child. She looked so small.

Another couple from New Life, Dave and Rocky

Kelly, came to wait with us during surgery. We prayed, talked and even laughed together, something I'm sure the other people in the waiting room couldn't understand. When the doctor emerged from the operating room, he asked if the Kellys were relatives. Without hesitating, my husband nodded. Jim didn't have to explain himself to me. Kristin's surgery only increased our understanding of the body of Christ. New Life was our family. Later, my mother even told me what an impact our church had on her.

Though the surgery revealed Kristin's cancer was treatable, there were no guarantees. As Jim went to get some sleep at the hospital boarding house, fear plagued me. How would Kristin respond to the chemotherapy? How could one little body withstand so much?

Sometimes scripture is like a kiss from heaven. The next morning, Dave read a passage from Deuteronomy 20 that strengthened us for an uncertain future. "When you go to war against your enemies and see horses and chariots and an army greater than yours, do not be afraid of them because the Lord your God, who brought you up out of Egypt, will be with you. Do not be faint-hearted or afraid; do not be terrified or give way to panic before them. For the Lord your God is the one who goes with you to fight for you against your enemies to give you victory."

The next weeks became a series of chemotherapy treatments and tests. We stayed in Omaha for a cycle of ten days, then returned again to Children's Hospital on the

third week. I quit my job. I had to be with my daughter, whatever the financial burden. I couldn't shake the fear that I could lose Kristin at any time, especially when she had to go under the knife again. This surgery was to remove the tumor from inside her spine.

Seeing the doctors with calculators, figuring the correct dosage of chemotherapy for Kristin's small body, was almost surreal. It broke our hearts to watch the chemicals pumped into her tiny frame. The pink color of the medicine was a stark contrast to the pink dresses and hair bows back home in Kristin's closet.

Even on our return trips to Kearney, "normal" life was far from normal. Kristin had a port installed in her chest for her medicines. Not only did I need to dress her wound, I had to inject heparin into the port so it wouldn't get clogged. When Kristin was put on stronger chemotherapy, a Home Health nurse came to our home. Any sickness could threaten our daughter. We washed our hands raw. When our son was exposed to chicken pox, Kristin and I had to move in with Al and Nancy Hammar, some church friends, for ten days until the danger passed. When we did go out, it was to church. Kristin had to be kept away from everyone. I can still see LaVonne Kinyon, Don Frank's mother, donned in a facemask, rocking my daughter in the balcony while I helped on the worship team.

Our faith became our refuge. We couldn't have endured the battle for Kristin's life without the body of believers at New Life. God carried us through our strug-

gle by using our family in Christ. They prayed for me
when I couldn't, and I stood on what they believed.

When the first MRI revealed no change in Kristin's tumor, the letdown was almost unbearable. The neu-
rosurgeon feared Kristin would not be able to use her legs.
But again, people from New Life visited us at Children's
Hospital and prayed us through the battle. They were so
sensitive to our needs, even bringing bath products for me.
I'll never forget sneaking away one day to an empty room
in the hospital and luxuriating in a long bath. For just a
moment, the sweet aromas took me to another world,
away from the antiseptic world in which we lived.

My stomach was in knots when Kristin went in for
her second MRI. The doctor told us not to be surprised if
we didn't see any change in the tumor. It was the perfect
setup for a miracle, but I couldn't see through the fog.
Even when the MRI showed the tumor had disappeared, I
couldn't feel excited. There was still exploratory surgery.
The surgeon couldn't believe it when he saw only scar
tissue from the previous surgeries. There was no evidence
of the cancer. Nonetheless, tissue was sent to St. Louis
for testing to be certain. My doubts forced me to my
knees. I had to learn not to focus on the circumstances,
but to focus on what God could do.

My hands shook when I heard the doctor's voice
come through our answering machine. There was no sign
of the tumor. Kristin was healthy.

During this trial, my husband would pray, "God,
don't let me waste the pain. Show me what You want me

to learn." As we walked through the valley of death, God taught us to trust Him, even when we couldn't see Him working. I don't understand all the "whys" behind our journey, but I do know that people watched our reaction during these dark days, and only God can know what seeds He planted. Kristin is now a teenager, and while she has some lasting side effects, including hearing loss, she is proof that our God still performs miracles.

Conclusion

By
Pastor Bob Wine

I trust at least a flicker of hope has been ignited within you, for either yourself or someone you know has faced similar, painful experiences. These stories are representative of many in our New Life family who have experienced genuine life change through a personal encounter with their Creator, God. If you have honest questions or doubts if such life-changing experiences are possible, each of us warmly extends an invitation to you to come and check out our church family. Freely ask questions, examine our reality factor, and if you choose, journey with us at whatever pace you are comfortable with. We just want you to know God is still completing the process of authentic life change in us, so we still make mistakes in our journey, like everyone will. Therefore, we acknowledge our continued need for each other's forgiveness and support.

If you are unable to be with us, yet you intuitively sense you would really like to experience such a life change, here are some fundamental essentials to consider. If you choose, at the end, say the suggested prayer. If your prayer genuinely comes from your innermost being, you can expect to experience the beginning stages of authentic life change, similar to those you have read about.

broken

- Acknowledge you have broken God's laws, and unless He forgives you, you will be forever separated form God. Romans 6:23: *"The reward for sin is death, but the gift that God freely gives is everlasting life found in Christ Jesus our Lord."* God's Word
- Believe in your heart God passionately loves you and wants to give you a new heart. Ezekiel 11:19: *"I will give them singleness of heart and put a new spirit within them. I will take away their stony, stubborn heart and give them a tender, responsive heart."* NLT
- Believe in your heart that, *"If you confess with your mouth that Jesus is Lord and believe in your heart that God raised Him from the dead, you will be saved."* Romans 10:9 NLT
- Believe in your heart that because Jesus paid for you breaking God's law, and because you asked Him to forgive you, He has filled your new heart with His life in such a way that He transforms you from the inside out. 2 Corinthians 5:17: *"When someone becomes a Christian, he becomes a brand new person inside. He is not the same anymore. A new life has begun!"* TLB

Pray this suggested prayer as if it was yours: "Lord Jesus, I know I am separated from You, but I want to change that. I am sorry for the choices I've made that have broken Your laws. I believe Your death paid for my sins, and You are now alive to change me from the inside out. Would You please do that now? Thank You for hearing and changing me. Now please help me know

Conclusion

when You are talking to me, so I can cooperate with Your efforts to change me." Amen.

We would love for you to come be a part of our family!

New Life Assembly
meets every Sunday
@
2715 W 39th St
Kearney, NE 68845-8243

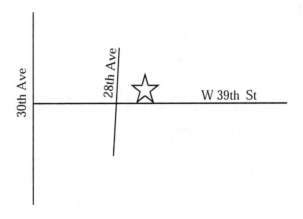

Or call us today at
308.234.1881

www.newlifekearney.org